I WOKE UP TO WORDS TODAY

I WOKE UP TO WORDS TODAY

DANIELLA DEUTSCH

atmosphere press

a letter to my reader

For most, looking at a map demonstrates structure. A path. Order. We look to maps for direction. Maps tell us: *This is how we get here.* Often, we feel confused and ask ourselves: *Where am I going?* We glance at a map and realize: *Ah, this is the way.* Maps give us answers. Maps guide us, support us, and we follow.

For me, a map of New York City catapults me into other-worldly trances. The lines are not only streets, but they are arteries to a body of life. The colors do not simply signify public transport but symbolize a deep rhythm. A beat. The ground is not only an island surrounded by bodies of water, but an organism so vast that I will spend my lifetime sinking my feet into it.

I admit to you with pure honesty, I am not from here. I migrated here. I mapped a course and found myself here. I came to connect with and unpack a new meaning of home here.

Looking at a map of New York City, I see the most powerful years of my life thus far. My past, my present, and my future dropped and dripped every which way. I see myself so clearly inside the concrete walls of my home. New York City is the only place I have ever felt my most authentic self. This city did not hesitate to build me inside of her, to include me, to nurture and nourish me, to catch me, and to propel me. I have vowed to digest every corner, and nobody here stops you from trying. As I stare at a map of New York City, I see myself. I feel alive. I see endless undiscovered cracks, moments waiting to be documented by a streetlight, fragments of my very own story, and particles of others – most of whom I will never meet.

Humans have always attempted to name their New York. Artists are constantly broadcasting the rhythm their New York sways to. Frank O'Hara's *Lunch Poems* tells the story of New York happening spontaneously – a New York viewed through the lens of a lunch hour. E.B. White's *Here is New York* is its own love letter to this city, one of profound essays dedicated to the way it changed after World War II. Craig Taylor chronicled New York City through voices – voices of strangers he met over the course of six years. He learned their stories and brought their voices to the forefront of how he chose to tell the frontline and under-appreciated story of New York City. And of course, Tom Wolfe once told me, "One belongs to New York instantly. One belongs to it as much in five minutes as in five years." So, here I write, narrating my New York through geographical poetry. My way of paying homage, in combination with deep self-reflection.

I look at the map and I know I left a strand of hair on 77th street when it was ripped off me during a spectacular embrace. I see my glimpses on the F train, L train, and Q train that strangers now own with my blessing. I see shoelace fuzz and elbow blood from a failed bicycle attempt in Tribeca. I see where I stupidly left a slice of trust on the corner of 14th street and 8th avenue. I see bitten off painted fingernails from late nights waltzing down Metropolitan Avenue as Patti Smith softly sings in my headphones. I see three milk cartons sitting on a rock in the middle of the street as we laugh on Hudson Street. I see the open invitation for anyone to finish the start of my smile on Pier 46. I see the spilled blueberries that likely remain in the impossible crevice of a booth on Avenue A. I see my spit mixed with many others all on the same rooftop on Wythe Avenue. I see my fingerprints brushed lightly on each book spine in the back of a store on Prince Street. I see the square of pavement where I crumpled on Valentine's Day and I see the rusting bridge where I soared on Labor Day. This is how I paint my New York, small details of me live inside the bones of the places my life played out. My story only feels whole alongside those coordinates.

Regardless of what occurs in my life, where I happen to be standing at that moment roots me there forever in my mind. The coordinates of my life are the main characters in both real time and in memories. I look at a map of my city and I can see strangers whom I will only shake hands with in my mind. That is what is so profound about this city. We find a way to connect with far more humans than we even actually know, simply by wandering the avenues. I leave a piece of me, visible and invisible, wherever I go here. This enthralling pattern has yet to occur anywhere else for me. Only here. This city asks me for me, pulls me apart and scatters me - each day making me more deeply engraved inside of her than I was before. For that, I thank her. For that, I bow down to her. For as triumphantly un-religious as I am, she has easily become my song, prayer, anchor, cross, and star.

As I continue to inhale the city into my bones, I feel as if I know my corners inside and out. However, I very well know that there are also secrets in this place I will never know, and this tiny island holds mysteries far beyond my clawing mind. Every human who dances in this city holds their own meaning to what the skyline whispers. Everyone here has their own eyes in which they see the city. They have their own version of the city, their own reality. Their own map. Their own story. I learn from yours; you learn from mine. And when we each fall asleep at night, my New York is not yours, and your New York is not mine. So, as I connect the dots of the city's skin with mine, I hope to one day find some way of paying homage to her.

On my darkest and most lonesome days, this city envelops me. Here, strength never fails to eventually emerge from me. The streets carry me. The buildings hover over me with fierce protection. New York City is a playground of striking solitude, yet it is also a place running rampant with fervent belief in human connection. It is unlike anywhere else on the planet. It makes me feel more alive than anything in the world. It is the reason I write to you today. It is my home, and I know I am not alone when I say New York City is my greatest love affair. Although I share her with millions more, she has a way of making me feel extraordinary every single day.

Find your coordinates, and they will be true to you.

Daniella

table of contents / my body's geography

to anyone still searching for your coordinates,
don't stop. they exist.

to blend oneself into a coordinate
requires a storming handful of solitude
a soft appetite for movement
and the instinct to find breath
between boroughs.

home

you led me to this godly city
to drink its holy water

dropped my hand
spun on your heel

and left me
with the greatest gift

each conversation with the avenues
began to spoon my empty lungs

and as my body grew into a map of New York
New York grew into a map of my body

so here I am rooted
your single scoop of failed devotion

birthed an undying allegiance
for my most glorious homeland.

Lights out. Eight million strangers go to sleep.

midnight on Avenue A

my American dream looks like
you. covered in my ashes. what
a fucking sight. to rise up from
our own slaughter, unarmed and
justly aware. perhaps without
much provocation. because in this
city, we bow. and lay our weapons
down to catch the weathered
bodies before they hit the catwalk.
we take care, you see. street tires
scream my name inside breathless
sirens. I swear I cannot be the only
one who hears it. they call me
towards a greater traffic light. one
that blinks blue. tangled in the
avenues. I kiss the cement. we are
intertwined as one artifact. you
are mine. a battleground and muse.

Devoción Coffee

the first half of my twenties,
I could not name myself. so I
spilled it out on the page, as
gore. when Toni Morrison was
asked why she likes to write so
much, she answered *'because
otherwise I'm stuck with life.'* I
too bleed out words. I cannot
shield myself from it. my internal
pages turn at tilt. peering through
the many faces who stare at my
thick brows, it is rare to find
someone as dear to me as a reader.
more so, one who on perhaps the
hottest day in August reminds me
that my heartbeat forms letters in
my sleep. life's momentum will
continue to erupt in art. to my
surprise, I am only a handful of
ink stains from whole.

Apartment 402

I am in love with a man I hate, it wears on
me. brings me to my knees with rapture
and misery. its company so sick, I swallow
the pill of devotion like breast milk. years
from now, my womanly insides will blink
out all of my youthful blindness towards
verifiable safety. an ally. the arms which
once welcomed hazardous pupils will one
day clasp sweetly on to steadfast eyelids.
and I swear to myself, my mind will rest.

Meatpacking District

I look up in time to see glistening
bodies as they make love with the
curtains open. for all of Manhattan
to see. sitting on tables and lying
on couches, bright and expensive
lights shine down. exposing skin
mixed with secrets mixed with
skin. they cut off the rest of the
Earth, opening windows and
unlocking doors. inviting me in to
feast on fingernails and shoulder
blades. laughing at the versions of
each other when they are dressed.
as their limbs become theatrical,
almost hysterical, they knock down
wall after wall. so if our city never
sleeps, I hear out their cries,
proving to the world they can
intertwine their bodies with
strength. with ease. with motion
and moments that are meant to be.
their bountiful declaration sings
out into my skull as if to say, *come
see us love! have a viewing party
and listen to us speak our language.
it exists. we exist.* and once their
sweet bodies have evaporated and
their solidarity has long since
vanished, they will do this again.
forever in their minds. always
making love with the curtains open.

the Q train

twenty something years old and my battery
recharges on the subway. I see you walk into
my car to ask a mere express line question.
in this moment you blend me into this city
almost as if I am not a transplant from three
thousand miles away. I foam at the mouth for
the city to see me the way I see me. how my
bones and breath match in a fucking beautiful
symphony with the sound of the sidewalks.
how I move in space amongst the buildings
as if they have been friends my whole life. the
way I watch the eight million people and
wonder, *what is your story?* knowing if I asked,
you would sit down to tell me. here, I am fed.
on the Q train, you look at me the way I look at
others. with burning questions. awe. sensuality.
taking one headphone out every few minutes,
you glance over. an attempt to converse. I am
busy putting on a show to seem more free
spirited than I truly feel today. a confidence
overwhelms me. we slam in without fear of eye
contact. stuck underground and boxed into our
minds. I would tear each brain open if I could. I
do my best to conquer you with my eyes. that is
what you are doing to me. I know because I have
mastered it. you make me feel unique. and alive.
that is how I view every damn New Yorker I lay
my eyes on. there is no city more spellbinding in
the world. you ask me when I am getting off. we
both ponder how it may feel to lock eyes and
exchange a weak secret. the invitation dangles in
the air, but I drop it. for what is this city without
a strand of mystery each day? you exit the car. I
turn my music loud and stare at someone else.

14th & 3rd Avenue, 7:45am

on despondent days, I rummage through
my brain and think of the silent communities
we belong to. they are both birthed and
buried inside divots and cones. under
lampposts and atop grates. cradled inside the
vascular streets of my mind, I see the young
man who waits for the M103 bus. he seems
close to my age. his green eyes appear far
younger than his boring ties. his weight
fluctuates throughout every winter and
summer. sometimes drastically. other times
not as much. whenever he gets a haircut, I
nod in approval. I nod to myself in approval.
once or six or so times I have imagined us
out for a drink. when his backpack changes
from linen to leather I take the liberty of
assuming he has been promoted.

restless on 6th Avenue

I want
to carve
you out
immaculately,
hold you
in my
hand,
and never
be made
to
creep
comb
or
wrestle
again

on the First Avenue L train platform

and just like that, my life changes on the
First Avenue L train platform. so does
yours - as if a love affair is only a miracle
for one party member. it is October. I slow
motion run to you, to be dramatic, of course.
as old friends, we embrace. as eventual
lovers, we take our collective first breath.
together, we board the train. three stops
West, three stops North. we step out at 72nd
Street. emerging side by side, your broad
frame is a mixture of safe and seductive. we
hold invisible cliff hangers with sturdy nets
in our cool palms. the others swarm us,
greetings of reunion and delight. soon
enough, no one else will matter. we cross
Amsterdam.

off Olive Street

I have become unraveled
by my young human heart.
fixated with 6am whispers
for the residents who will
one day enter these walls
after we leave. I am sorry
we crumbled the beams
and shattered the
floorboards. please craft
a better home for yourself
here. I promise to do the
same in my mind.

990 Washington Avenue

botanical gardens used to empty me
out. scramble up my organs and leave
me with only a desperate phone call,
begging to understand how anyone
can survive a 90-degree summer with
no one to sweat with. but then, flowers
decided to grow inside me. thirsty for
my sweet perspiration. crawling from
the dirt between my toes into my never
still and very open heart.

a kitchen in Alphabet City

it's a Thursday and I seem to have misplaced
your eye color in my mind. I blink, and wine
freezes in my mouth under my tongue. I wrestle
to trap it, but a drop slips towards the back,
taunting me. most likely as if to say *it's gone,
he's gone, you know that.* I swallow it with
tension, the way you do when you are
aggressively alone. these thousand dollar
walls box me into solitude, as if I need a
reminder. so I console myself, voicing to the
spoons and the sausages that I surely chose
for the liquid to escape. and truthfully, I may
never catch up to my own nostalgia. blue eyes
consume me, green eyes betray me, brown
eyes blind me. and if I called you to remind
myself, sank my teeth into the slippery past to
hear your answer, I may not even believe you.

125th Street, Harlem

you ask me
why? why here?
I tell you plainly, without the seasons
I do not

          die

by that I mean to say

                I cannot bloom

or s t r e t c h

or

c

    r

       a

         c

           k

I will not walk nearly far enough
on my own skeleton's

      tightrope

or sink deep enough
into the archive of my veins
to   rummage for the

rebirth

I so desperately   thirst for.

Metropolitan Avenue

I smelled your towel tonight.
the pink one that still hangs
in our bathroom. it has not been
washed yet. I do not ever want
it clean. I bury my face and
breathe you in. I begin to cry.
I want to cry harder. for longer.
something chokes me and I cannot.

Bedford & North 4th

the corner of Bedford and North 4th means
nothing to me for 521 days. until suddenly,
it does. the sweetness of the time between
crashing into you and becoming one with
you lingers for longer than a sun cycle. it is
April when the pavement freezes from us. it
sits patiently for an eventual transformation.
it halts for the sublime. the cement heartbeat
pulses inside the borough's spring air. sidewalks
carry far more heavenly knowledge than us
Earthly creatures can prophesize. there is
something both soothing and devastating about
the oblivion of a story's beginning. how is it we
so rarely know when our lives are being carved
into the ground's history? a patch of pavement
may first appear mundane. until suddenly, it is a
character in our world. a different corner turned
becomes a different life lived. I fantasize about
the places my heels have already brushed. I
imagine the air above awaiting my newest story.
often, our bodies plant seeds in the neighborhood's
cracks to grow and nurture for a later day – flaming
with meaning only time will reveal. I can faintly
hear the songs. yet I do not know who calls me, the
sirens or the muses. today I return to the corner of
Bedford and North 4th, as a veteran. I smile, looking
for the stories being written at this very moment.
how many future tales dangle in the frozen summer
air? where will my next Bedford and North 4th be?

from my small East Village couch

on the precipice of a wailing time machine, I cradle
my blistered heart as it ruptures with notable silence.
it is no staggering surprise my eye sockets collapse
under the weight of warmth. humanity bleeds out of
me a color from another constellation. I still find myself
pulling out from a long season of unmatched decency.
every damn day. I could cross a bridge with the promises
I still carry in my back pocket. and surely there is
something noble about a mouth full of wanting.

May on the Pulaski Bridge

here is where we get to be lost—
although I do admit there are
muted moments trapped inside
myself where I crave living so
entirely and so forcefully. I fear
it will foolishly break me too soon.

Orchard Street

over french fries
on Orchard Street
I reveal to you
my plan
to rip open
and split open
my whole damn
life at twenty-three
a brief five months
of knowing me
you dip a fry
into aioli
take my hand
across the table
pay the check
and journey on
to show me
a slice of
female allegiance
I have not known
in a very long time

JFK

I cried the entire 2,475 miles it took
to leave you behind. I did not wipe
away a single tear all 342 minutes.
they streamed and dropped
and puddled on the seat between
my legs. a pool of my own cracked
and achy displacement. like a sad
shrine to my approaching sense of
wandering. a pilgrimage I never
chose to make. and now I am trying
to explain to myself how it feels
inside my somewhat refined bones
to return to you. or at least how I
imagine it will be. I am not quite yet
on my way. nevertheless the wheels
go up—

256

out of the ashes
births the labor
of
nonlinear
learning
smeared with
seeds of
clinking competence
from the dancing
cinders
climbs and claws the
work
for I became accustomed
to breathing
inside this crowded map
alone
you know you're not the
only one
who loves this city, don't
you?
his whispers bathe
me
we are tracing my
film reel outline
and I sink
deeper to my knees
every day
rewriting
this twirling borough

Hanover Square

you ate up all my dreams last night.
I am amazed it did not kill me. shocked
at my own muscle to rip myself from
your gaze, I am left to collect my
fragmented desires in the land of awake.
I drag them through the streets. cold
and unrequited. at least the crosswalks
will hold me for a bearable moment.
closely in their arms. to inhale the
alliance I now find myself begging for.

you are always here

> *"And what kind of madness is it anyways, to be in love with*
> *something constitutionally incapable of loving you back?"*
> (*Maggie Nelson, Bluets*)

whenever I drink, I just want to cry and make love
to you. write sermons for you. scratch every itch of
you. tonight, I find myself limp on the corner of a
park between 53rd and 54th. or perhaps it's 52nd.
god knows how I got here but I know I'm exhausted.
I must have jumped out the window, or maybe I
crawled. yet you are always here. and in truth, I am
having trouble thanking you. for your body is purified
cement, your lips are 3am neon bulbs. to applaud you
would be too effortless a motion. your hair drips dirty
snow down your railway back. your eyelashes blink
out first time cigarette butts. please invite me over.
your eyes are filled with spray paint for my careless
tonsils to gulp. your ankles sing of the beloved graveyard
shifts. I fear I will never please you well enough. your
nose is crafted from hot salami and celebratory smashed
glass. your fingertips bleed the cool three minutes before
the relief of a summer downpour. it is no secret that I
think of you when we are apart. your stomach is lathered
in shadows of the sky. your back speaks languages
untranslatable. I promise to be your greatest and most
grand affair, don't you see? I will strip naked and kiss your
roots, wash myself with your soot and candy. yesterday a
woman on the A train gave me a stale look, as if to say *don't
get too carried away.* who would be foolish enough to make
such a promise? but do know, I will never leave you. one
day, my love for you will be buried in your very own bones.

Apartment 1B

how strange and momentarily
maddening, you will never
know the feeling of your hands
on my body. and I cannot
embrace the feeling of my hands
on your body. there is a secret
language concealed inside just
one palm. a delicacy fed only to
the receiver. we wash our skin
with touch and are left to imagine
the chills of our own power. after
all, Brooklyn has never been shy.

Lower East Side shame

I am speaking directly to you as I recall how you
stepped back on the map and did not tell me.
I am looking right at you while my limbs cannot
shake how you crashed into our former lair and
chose to slink into the shadows. after planting an
oath of civility on my shivering tongue, just faint
enough for me to swallow my entire life without
considering abandoning your pledge. instead, you
stole a city corner for yourself for the weekend.
I can see you now. traipsing through the streets
you brought me to, with cowardice. leaving me
with a blade thrust so deeply in me I almost lost
my taste. my touch. my sight. did you forget this
town is tiny? or did you simply remember our
truths too starkly to face the demons you had
once sprinkled through the crosswalks?

14th & 3rd Avenue, 7:45am

rummaging further in between
the overpasses of my mind, my
silent communities include the
woman who walks her two great
Danes. she always has one crucial
strand missing from her ponytail.
she turns my morning breath
melancholic if I stare for too long.
one dog is white with black spots.
the other is a chocolate brown.
they pull her along like they are in
charge. she easily surrenders. the
canines tug her into the day as if
she has no true direction. she
probably doesn't.

the market on North Third

it is early wintertime. I leave to get us rosemary.
I run to the market on North Third. tonight, it
is the one missing ingredient. I refuse to make
my dish without rosemary. every detail counts
when you make food like you are making love.
every bite must be entirely fleshed out, full of
the flavors it deserves. it is no wonder rosemary
is often associated with Aphrodite. I hurry to the
store, as if places in this city are not open all night.
I answer a phone call from my grandmother with
my free hand as I step through the entryway. as
we talk, I realize quickly I cannot find rosemary
anywhere. I wander the aisles. I search the racks
as I continue to speak with my grandmother. in
the spice aisle, my lips surprise me as they casually
form the words, *you know, I think I may have
found my person.* she says, *oh, I very much think
you have.* I smile to the Ba–Tampte garlic dill
pickles. and then, there it is. low on the ground in
a small pot. my eyes lock in on it. I gasp, *I would
have never looked there!* my grandmother replies,
for him? quickly hanging up, I run for the last
rosemary bush. underneath canned beans, a peculiar
placement. I exhale, the herb in my arms. now my
dinner will be whole. as I check out, the woman
at the register says to me *rosemary, huh? the
symbol of remembrance.*

I realized I loved you on the FDR

I could sit sputtering. clinging
to my own tunnel vision of
persecution. disappearing into
a hollow city of my own damn
interrogations. instead, I say,
flood my lungs with bergamot
and mahogany. medicinal and
hardy. trip me over and melt
me artfully. I gaze as my insides
drip like candle wax. burning
my core at both ends. although
may I be so bold as to name it
timeless. creatures like us do
not simply wake up one day
and feel at home with another
set of palms. yet a pleasurable
surprise suspends me. I learn
the mountains ground me. sway
me sideways with certitude and
carve me out. at last I cave. and
climb from enchainment to light,
an edge I am willing to plunge from.

farewell to the West

my words mean something

                               here
for they are born

                               here

I was not born here
I am not from here

yet my words claim the

t
      i
            t
                l
                      e

of starting

                    here

and
finishing   here

to all of those who

      told me my body
      and my words
      are one in the
         same

that it makes no difference for flesh to be

g r o w n

here   as long as it is

nurtured   here
I thank you and

         I hold you dear to me.

I never considered my own death until the corner of 1ˢᵗ and 14ᵗʰ

I never considered my own death until
the corner of 1st and 14th. a deep luxury,
I am acutely aware. I never considered my
own death until I slugged my slim five-foot-
five frame home, on a frigid March evening.
pausing in front of the subway to wipe an
icy tear and inspect my own existence. I
was twenty-three years old. my ancient
pathways clouded with shame. any
recognition of myself had already slipped off
the bone, bowing out with a cruel curtsey. my
stunned heart filled with a fear of future
missed connections, as I braced myself for the
steep hill I saw seeping into view. who do we
become when our identity is proven wrong?
how do we throw ourselves back into living
when the last toss split us in half? what do we
believe in when we stop speaking the tongue
we were thought to be fluent in? the corner of
1st and 14th left me in a daze of my tumbling fate.
pulling the pistol's trigger for a marathon I did
not have any desire to train for. when a dark
hole of unexpecteds collapses into you, you
quickly realize you do not ever want to exit this
Earth with even a shadow of *maybes*.

inspired by a passage from E.B. White's
Here is New York

I am sitting at the moment in a
210 square foot apartment. the
price we pay for the lunatic, yet
unconditional care we have for
this damn place. we renew this
care year after year, despite cost
and fatigue, because it is a
liberation unlike any other. we
flaunt it. we are here to stay. I am
43 blocks from where Billy Joel
recorded his fifth studio album,
The Stranger, at A&R Recording
studios, 11 blocks from Katz Deli,
where Rob Reiner's mother spoke
the famous line, *I'll have what
she's having.* 67 blocks from where
Jeffery Epstein was arrested in his
Upper Eastside townhouse, 3 blocks
from St. Mark's Church where Patti
Smith gave her first ever poetry
reading. 46 blocks from where
Charles C. Ebbets shot the iconic
photograph of construction men on
their lunch break while building
Rockefeller Center. 12 blocks from
where Marsha P. Johnson bravely
began the Stonewall Riots. and I do
believe there will be more history
to seep into the cracks between
where I sit and where I write. but
for now I wait. for life to cycle
around and on top and below and
all over me.

Grand Street

Friday night and she sits at the sushi bar
sipping her glass of ruby red wine by
herself. I took one abnormal psychology
class, so I'm diagnosing her with loneliness.
my big head tries to read through her pretty
skull. wondering what could have happened
that she must dip her tempura into their
house made soy sauce, without any company.
six months later I am telling lies to my loved
ones so I can slip out the door, alone. and bask
in the incomparable silence of a glass of red
wine with myself on a glorious Friday night at
the sushi bar.

March on Madison

forty flights up and two fire
escapes later we dangle. off
the edge of the world. more
so we dangle off the edge of
99th street but I am not so
sure there is much of a
difference. we stand in
conversation with the clouds.
although the sky appears to
foster only a few tonight. we
twirl our eyes through the
tiny model streets below.
blinking to make out a taxicab
or a coffee stand. a hush
tumbles through the winter air
for us tonight, landing on this
island and atop my mind. we
are lit up strictly by somewhat
purposeful pockets of glow
mixed with our shy breath. I
plant myself inside a long-
standing moment. the luxury
of evaporating from true time
to peer downward at our lives
below swallows us for the night
with glorious quietude.

underground

grates shake
and dance

        atop

the 472 subway stations we have grown here
sirens never fail to do us the favor of

      drowning out

woeful longings
for the one we best not see again

men

        scream

up into the night
a frenzy they hardly understand themselves

women grow

    louder

each day
and sing
deep blue
to be seen

drills pound and scrape
for a newer
shinier tomorrow

coins make a

        home

inside bent over cups
shaken and stirred for a glimpse of a

metamorphosis

the sounds here leak a wealth of
infinite commotion
we bleed

      havoc

yet inside my blood flow
I am

still

serenity is an underground gala

I am

            unwavering

quietude is an above ground beat
I inject the

      lunacy

into my veins
and cradle it with

                        motherhood.

off Havemeyer

tonight is poetry. amber and
smoke. candlelit and wet with
breath, a delicate creation.
there is an ease inside this
touch. a devoted cadence. to
think I was blind to your
tongue, deaf to your eyes.
dangled in the rearview for
misspent years. I reel. now, our
page sings. a bud, growing flames
and exhaling courage. I close my
eyes, gift you my back to trickle
your words down. our love holds
the momentum of the bridge that
writes my nights. you whisper,
there will be art about you.

table 23, Flatiron

after couples
counseling they
devour Italian
food next
door, the
identical spot
each week,
waltzing through
and as
they swallow
their wine
hers, red
his, white
they speak
a language
of reminiscence
on how
in this
city we
all slip
into different
versions of
ourselves to
be safe
yet also
to be
soldiers

nothing truly dies in Hell's Kitchen

when I need to be part of something far greater than myself, I sprinkle my words through the cracks in the streets. gifts for the underworld to inhale. I ration out my above ground saga for the alternate deserving half below. where invisible minds screech and past lives are gladly buried. for this city has glistening layers only the true escapists can conjure back up. yet I hear each vocal chord, burning hot. still palpably alive. they are all trickled through the bricks, the rubber and mold. aching to be recalled. to be regrown. I feel pounding fists at my heels, as if it is my duty to preserve it all. so here I find myself again, in conversation with those who mapped out their bodies around the city long before now. can you hear me? I am content without the answer.

Prospect Place

I follow my strung-out dream,
bursting with curious ammunition.
I am convinced you feel my outline,
as any decent New Yorker would.
if you hear me swallow at every
turn, I am grateful for your humble
silence. you interpret my desires as
an act of healing over harm. before
I know it, I am tapping at your wicked
window with my mind. I break
through the pillars. inside crooked
walls, my guts fill with a slush of
scenes. this home houses: whiskey,
sweat, blood, coffee, semen, tears,
snot. I cup my hands in front of my
weakened eyes and drain the life of
your sweetest days. returning home, I
swallow my boring spit, chew out my
brain for one last vignette and step
away. barely missing a pothole.

sweet hour facing North 5th

we face the sun. we hear nothing.
a sweet hour to pause. a gift we
place on each other's tongues and
spines, one others often overlook.
some days, we are miraculously
compelled to breathe in this patch
of rumbling animation. there are
moments when we sit to the side of
this cacophony of spun-out existences.
it is the late afternoon, and we hold
the air around us. soaking in warm
bones and softness. we sip Adrianne
Lenker and Mary Oliver. do not forget
to recline in this city. when sunlight
streams in and casts a shadow on the
wall, always lie down and become one
with the shapes. all else can wait.

we cry everywhere in New York

there is a human person crying

                  inside

each avenue of this hardened city

              a separate sidewalk world

with those who live and love to scratch

emotional
i t c h e s

and tear off the scabs with premature   smiles
we breathe in tumultuous
             air
                         with
                         elitism

and exhale it out with a strand of outstanding

pride

does it turn you on in the very same way?

c a t c h i n g   sodium
                from strangers

                we will never know
                on blurry corners

every inch of negative space extends a faithful arm

                            for this city is a love letter
                            to deeply invisible energy

wrapping us all
up
just to spit us   out again

this cult of tears   follows   me with tortuous   obsession
so tell me

when we disappear into our pain here,

where is it we go?

Jane Street

my teeth hit your teeth in the middle of the West Village.
and by that I mean, we kiss with eruption. our initial slam
is likely the most of each other we will own. a nearby stranger
in my ear hisses *what would this city be if we weren't here to
fill it?* I touch a lot of teeth, you know. I spend a lot of nights
on fire in these dirty mid 20s. just this minute I see a
cockroach, as I come into the pain of having nothing left to
say. swallowing over how I cry differently now. and I often
forget to blink. my brain swims inside brick walls. I sit,
crammed. and bathe in lazy temptation. I am not heartbroken
by him, believe me. I am heartbroken by the idea in which I
could have been heartbroken by him.

Graham Avenue

is it really running

                        away
                        if we find a home

i   n   s   i   d   e   the

            wreckage?

Hammerstein Ballroom

following a tide of darkness
the lights come up in the middle
of 34th street. and leaping out
of a night of voices and rhythmic
sensation, you all hold me from
every angle. suspended, just long
enough to grasp the reins. the night
dances a blurry tango. yet somehow,
I recall every moment. I am left
swooning, sweating, galloping, and
nourished. song is the language of
sadness. but it is also the story of
being alive. my world pauses beneath
beams of streaked colors. my cup
runs over, and I swear to squeeze it
and spread it well. and slowly in the
days to follow I will store away this
feeling in my veins and drag the
ballroom back with me for eternity.
in all honesty, a hot spring night is a
fucking miracle in itself.

Maspeth Avenue

sitting on the edge of a rusting bench
I recall how

      I lost all my innocence
      on top of you

      in one singular night

I

climbed on
your bare and
longing chest
p r e s s e d   my

      weight
      into your hips
and handed over my purity
with

                  pride
                  gusto
                  beauty

letting go of years of curiosity
and bliss

from up above
I straightened my back
t o s s e d my hair over   and around
to look down at

      you

the one inside of

      me

the night I released my youth

leaping through a plane of
                                        womanhood

you stared up at me,
            childlike
yet your voice boomed

                                        the man
                                        who would teach
                                        me
                                        all I needed
                                        to know

yet today, I remember
looking

            down towards your eyes

it was you who needed all I had to offer
and for pages on   pages   of my life

I would continue to offer
and to
r
            i
                        s
                                    e

and repeat
always climbing on top

to demonstrate
to test
to sacrifice
to endure the high road
to guide your blind nature

                        you believed you were the teacher

even in the moment you were altering me
in truth I was showing you a fragment of my

            future strength

a small taste
of my talents in taking   c h a r g e
when you could not muster up the
might

or ever master   the care.

a revelation in traffic on Norfolk Street

I do not swallow promises. I train myself
in my sleep. if I may deliver one restless
strand of unsolicited counsel: do not ever
beg to be loved. do not sway. do not whine.
do not grovel. do not persuade. it is a low
and wretched pit to outwardly pray your
lover can scrape the will to leave off their
tongue. there are bursting rooms filled for
you of open palms and effortless allegiance.

a hotel room on Ludlow

I dreamt last night you told me you were sick
(I forgot you could appear there). in my weary
unconscious mind, you turn to me with grid
locked eyes to repeat your fear you are falling
ill. now I may be ill too. you say you feel a fever
running through you. *check my back to see the
sweat*, you say. *just a summer cold*, I assure
you. I brush Worry underneath us both. yet
the fool is me, for Worry will not be brushed.
Worry drips and leaks like sweat with nothing
to blot it out. Worry has thighs and ankles and
toes to run fast. fevers tumble through us and
gain sly momentum the longer we do not see the
sweat. *just a summer cold,* I say again. you shake
your head low. a century ago, just a summer cold
could lay a man down on his deathbed.

a window seat

I blink

      once

my city looks small
how mild the world

      feels   from

               here

silence beats effortlessly as I

 e m p t y out the

         sanest
           crevices

of me

dumping it to the   curb

shuttering out permanence

         do not get me wrong

I am not surrendering

    I am
    wavering

between here and

      history.

14th & 3rd Avenue, 7:45am

I think of the tiny grandfather who
brings his granddaughter to grade
school each morning, clearly always
running late. they speed walk. hand
in hand, too afraid to let go. even if
it will quicken the pace of the journey.
I see the young university student
with high socks and sandals and a
sweatband who never fails to walk in
the city bike lane. somehow he always
appears as if he has been up all night
having sex for the very first time.

Apartment 12

I cut my knee running out the door the
last night I saw you. horizontal. on my
left leg. I searched half-heartedly for a
bandage, no luck. *let me bleed* I thought.
it will stop eventually. today is eventually.
my air conditioner is broken, and I listen
to Pharoah Sanders and pick at the scab
to drag out the reminiscence of you. the
night I stained blood in the bathtub was
the last time my body would sit in that
marble. at least sometimes I leave behind
what wounds me. now the next tenants
complain of a mess. on the contrary, my
new bathtub is sparkling. stainless. today
is a beginning, one I did not ask for.
nevertheless, a beginning. *how does it
feel?* well, my knee scar is healing. my
body is leagues ahead of me. and I think I
found a bandage a moment ago.

Second Avenue

here I am, hello. held once more by the city. only
this time, I stand sixteen flights up. again, I rely
on her cacophony of sounds. she cradles me in
her arms. I find my seat with ease — I nod in
salutation. like clockwork, I fall sideways into the
abyss. I let it take me and swallow me and pet me.
an inertia I do not fight, yet I will not succumb to
it. I choose to be here. to break and to mend here.
I choose to proclaim this city as my fellow hero. I
pity the ones who never shake her hand. she will
pull you close to her chest, like a mother. ask and
she will open. it is a rarity to find a belief so steadfast
in such a fiercely unreligious human such as me. yet
here I am. tall and still, here.

Manhattan Bridge at sunset

I want

        someone
to feel
about me
the way

        I feel
        about
this
city,

        addicted
        and

        unafraid.

exchanging grief on 11th Street

in the blazing Wednesday sun, two women
exchange grief. a few steps in front of a
bakery that has fed the block for 127 years,
they both carry a lighter load of composure
today. this is no crime. on another plane of
time, the heat mixes with glee. yet in this
plane of time, hours amongst the desolate
move as mud. the two women dangle their
stinging sentences on the paint splattered
corner. they catch each other's woes. they
pocket the damage with ease. the passersby
disintegrate and the noises retreat. casting
a shielded arena for the two women to fold
up their weighted organs. to roll their
sorrows onto affirming eyes. they nod at how
grief answers to many different names, yet
pain undoubtedly sings a similar heartbeat.
sometimes, a simple *I see you* is all we need
to cross the street on a blisteringly hot
afternoon in New York – at least without
tripping over our own fired up life.

Houston

I pass *The Library*, off Houston. two summers ago
you bought me a Stella at the graffitied bar. I was
wearing polka dots. this summer, we broke each
others hearts in the height of a heatwave. all I was
wearing was your shirt, nothing else, when we
crumbled. ninety-four fucking degrees. sweat mixes
well with tears, clever. now my newest walls know
only a shattered me. they have only met a grieving
me. they must sigh and think, *what have we gotten
ourselves into?* hands over my face and a slight a
choking sound: signals to my downpour. *here she
goes again.* I tell my walls, I am sick of me crying too!
and it has only been 12 feeble days. I still have six
stages of grief left, my god. I plan to live a long life.
I hope for at least sixty or so more years. today
my clock reads twenty-six. I have never been good
at math but that seems like a lot of mornings to
wake up without each other, no? I apologize to my
walls. when I am not crying, I am writing. and when
I am not writing I do laundry to cleanse my tear-
soaked pillowcases. I am wasting quarters that could
be for gumballs. to freshen my breath to kiss someone
new. quarters for buying myself a Stella. instead, I
build my own library, color coding my books. I wear
more polka dots, and I get a record player. I just
cannot listen to that one album - you know the one.
Houston haunts me. so I hang art piece after art piece
on my walls to shield them from the viewing party of
my inconsolable hours. and I promise my ceiling there
is more to me than what they have witnessed in this
sticky pre hurricane heat.

91 Third Avenue

I test the carbon steel blade. I recall
over and over how you badgered
me. how you warned me, playfully.
how you widened your eyes and
wagged your finger. instilling in me
how I must sharpen my knives. a
chef's most trusted companion. *if
they are dull, they will find a way to
cut you.* the interior of this stupid
store is humid. *treat them with care,
or they will slice you.* the aisle is clear,
I brush the tip with my thumb. *and
don't let them soak, they'll lose their
edge.* I press my finger slowly down,
hard. what I can tell you, is that there
is no amount of sharpening my god
damn knives I could have ever done
to defend myself from this anguish. it
was never going to be a blade inside a
drawer to ruin me. all the unsharpened
knives in the world could not slip and
wound me the way you have. yet here I
am. adopting knives to care for. I cannot
place the reason it matters, or even how
I wandered here. my knives could all
rust out and you would never know.
perhaps it is the companionship. of the
blades in the dark. and knowing I have
held far worse demons in my hands.

a thought while drinking coffee on Irving

city sounds have always
put me to sleep. yet on
occasion when they do
not, I lie in bed and think
what I would say at
your funeral if you died.

the place that knows too much

I speed walk to the train, with every logical intention
of going West. I am late. I shamelessly crawl under
the turnstile, and my body memory plays a trick on
me. leaping onto the departing train, I sigh. the doors
close, I feel the lurch in a strange direction. my mind
catches up. we speed East. my muscles have dragged
me towards the wrong river, I do not blame them. I
have knighted this borough as home more than any
other. so I take the fortuitous ride. I do not particularly
want to, but I am already halfway to the ghost town of
me. emerging above ground, my eyes close. I hear myself
mutter, *this part of the city knows too much.* I am not
wrong. this neighborhood carries far more of me than
the others. here is riddled with feverish tales of
dependence, and is chronicled with days of righteous
empowerment. here I have seen the waterfront through
every season. here I have sweated through the most
brutal summer heatwaves, and here I have been chilled
to the bone by the iciest winter of the last decade. my
mind spins, and I relinquish control over where my
body walks me. I activate. I am on overdrive. 60.71
million square feet and 151,308 residents, which only
I would care to research. here I have written hundreds
of pages. here I have made countless hours of love.
here my so-called mermaid hair has caught on fire,
twice. here I have said goodbyes and hellos. here I have
inked my body, thrice. a handful of the darkest nights of
my life dangle as ghosts here. undoubtedly some of the
brightest days of my life were birthed here. I survived
here. I healed here. over and over again on these streets.
I mended from you. and you. from me. layers of my spine
are etched into the sidewalks, old monologues sit on
rooftops. each block filled to the brim with breathtaking
skeletons. every direction and I bump into another me. I
shake each of her delicately brave hands. perhaps, I will
stay a while.

Kings County

I cannot remember if I made your bed on my way out.
my mind replays both scripts. each are distinctly
believable. in one, I abandon the ritual. I do not pull the
covers to the edge. frankly, I scorn at the tired mattress.
it appears worn from the weight of our messy minds –
imagine how we feel. the pillows spill out. the duvet
sinks partly to the floor, slinking away from the night of
failed love making and the morning of sorrow. in another
script, tradition flows from my fingertips. I dance precision
and care from my belly, leaning over the wooden frame to
polish off the job. I made the bed through four seasons, it
would be wrong to leave without one final touch. I smooth
out the wrinkles. one last gesture. perhaps an attempt to
tuck in the ghosts of us for sleep, one final time.

Grand Central

the last time I stood beneath the gold and green
tinted constellation ceiling, I believe I wore a
turtleneck. your blue mask matched the cover
of the book I had promised to bring you. we
stood adjacent from the 108-year-old clock. she
watched our vibrating outlines part ways after a
misty day of genesis. I swear the hands chimed
for us. as I walked away, I carried Joan Didion
in my backpack. you held Maggie Nelson safe
in your raincoat pocket. today I blink and I am
here again, beneath Orion's belt. sometimes we
must rewrite the coordinates to save us from
going over the edge. this is how my mind works.
I board a train, I do not know which one. it does
not matter, send me in any direction.

pavement

every body
draped
in
stories,
I hoard.

an ode to fallen coordinates

she invites me to close my eyes. to bring myself
to my calmest space. where I am safe. my mind
darts to coordinates I do not appear at any longer.
I file the room behind other candidates. yet the
room saunters back and taps me on the shoulder,
pouring into my brain and seeping down my neck.
just to the base, landing right where I breathe from.
I have forgotten to breathe. these four walls are not
mine, they were never mine. they are now fallen
coordinates. Ruth Padel told me, *the past is not where
you left it*. nonetheless, I have seldom felt more at
home than this 1901 building. oddly enough, I cannot
recall if you spoke that sentiment or if I did. it is now
all a spotted mixture of fire tangled memories, alive
only in my wide mind. perhaps both can live out loud –
the death of a space I once danced in, spinning with the
knowledge that the dance was truly a graceful one. I sit
inside. I am on your bed. it is partly made, with the
darker set of sheets. they are newly clean. I breathe. the
softness underneath me is a blend of gentle and secure,
tender enough to lend an ear to countless clusters of
stories. young enough to hold them calmly. there are at
least four shades of wood, all who converse with one
another. the hexagon sings to the rectangle. they inhabit
close, but kind quarters. I breathe. glass window panes
spread above and across, an invitation to always look out
and live. light knows to stream in and touch us when we
need it most. benign beasts stare down, with fierce
protection of the walls. the many sets of eyes tell me they
have seen more than they care to discuss, and that they
are content with holding that wisdom close to them. I do
not argue. Richard McGuire sits proudly on top of Tao Lin
on top of that bright red one with the bodies. Cashmere
and Peruvian cotton are tucked away, with stories of your
mother folded up inside. yellow squares hold their tongues
open, ready for the Sakura Pigma Manga ink to color their
short-lived lives. beeswax candles melt sideways as
Fuubutsushi trickles from the speakers. empty plant holders
quietly wait to be impregnated, empty notebooks sheepishly
wait to be given a chance. I breathe. then, I remember with

tolerant solace you are no longer a tenant of this space. the months somersaulted into the fall, and I am sure you already returned the key. I never saw the room empty. I never sat amongst the bones. I choose to remember it as it was before, whole. alive. awake and lived in. with the faint smell of chamomile, peach, and ceramic happily lingering. it is an amusing thing to appeal for ownership of a place solely animated inside one's mind. I open my eyes.

Thompson Street

my jaw clenched so tightly I had to
flee the city, imagine that. pressure
down my spine from tensing in the
dark. my upper neck fighting off any
more crowded dreams, like the one
I had on Ludlow. we rent a car on
Thompson Street. my almost six-foot
tall twin flame takes the wheel for me,
as she has been doing now symbolically
for months. it is no failure to pine for
fresh air. it is no betrayal to back up and
into the woods, despite allegiance to the
metropolitan glow. sometimes you have
to re-introduce yourself to this city. not
only to stay whole, but to feel intact. she
will always shake your growing hand, again.

a sidewalk conversation

I told the streets, I think the world has returned
to beat poetry. my words crack down on the
sidewalk fast these days. or perhaps I have just
begun to feel the world letting me open my mouth
to my mind again. something this city not only
allows for, but sits and begs and begs for.

the Jitney stop, 44th Street

I saw your bus today. well, not your bus
per se. the bus you brought to life. the
one you chose the colors for: the light
purple, pink, and orange. the bus you
stayed up late into the night for, clenched
your fists for, held your breath for. I saw
it leave the 44th Street stop. I chased it as
far as I could handle, my long brown hair
sweeping across my face as I sprinted. you
loved my middle part. surely there were at
least thirty strangers on the bus, all held by
your design. deep in their own lives, unaware
of the man who chose the lettering. the one
who detailed the gradient. they simply ride
East. I feel they have the privilege of being
inside of a small part of you. unknown to
them, they are in conversation with you. a tall,
olive-skinned young artist. with a specialty in
lithography, but a paycheck from advertising.
I cannot blame them for their ignorance, how
are they to know? the purple, pink, and orange
fade away, yet you painted my colors eternally.
the riders may speed off in your creation, but I
can still feel your body deep inside of mine. I
walk the other way - home. I saw your bus
today. I wonder if you could feel it in your bones.

14th & 3rd Avenue, 7:45am

the bridges of my psyche spell out the
long island thick accented mom with
twins who wears her weighted down
leopard coat year-round. her heels get
higher for every year her kids inch up
closer to her height. the boy appears
protective of his sister. he holds no
concept yet of how the world will
behave shockingly differently towards
them. I imagine the man with a radiant
smile who takes my bagel order 212 days
a year. he went to Florida last winter for
three weeks to see his family. he had not
seen them in four years. he warned me,
sweetly. nonetheless no one spreads the
perfect proportion of cream cheese on
my bagel the way he does.

from my large East Village couch

I read you, you read me. the
room has a quiet vibrato.
you mention my commitment
to coordinates. *your latitude
and longitude.* in this moment,
they are my home. it is pouring
out my window and my right
hand flies up to my chest, in
preparation. my left hand holds
my belly, a maternal instinct
towards my exposed self. I rock
there, contemplating the
limitations of my own courage
(later on I learn your heart
was pounding just as fast). my
left leg went numb two or nine
minutes ago – I only now find
myself shifting my weight beneath
the emerald velvet sofa to relieve it.
I wish to cradle myself. instead, I
drop my shoulders and slow my
panting. I sip in air, inhaling relief.
I catch my thoughts, along with
my spit. I am not in pain. I am but
a jumbled mix of what it is to be
alive. and to have somewhat of a
unique definition of it tonight.

my mirror corner

everything makes me think of you. you are indelible.
I hear you in jazz music, I smell you in hot coffee. I
taste you in spacious kitchens and small art galleries.
I feel you inside of green sweaters and glasses of fine
wine. I see you in clean ceramics and oceanic animals.
you are inside morning and night. you are fresh pasta,
golden hour shadows, and well-tended to candles. but
when I look in the mirror, all I see is Me. I pass an
ownerless mirror on the street on my walk to work,
each day. there is not one crack. I find myself returning
back to this mirror on the street, over and over. even
when it is not on my route – my mirror corner. I peer
through the glass, to ground me in myself. to lock eyes
with my eyes, a practice I am not even sure I recommend.
it is revealing to connect the dots of my internal world to
the external characters of mundane objects and places.
an attempt to leave yours behind. a ritual to wipe away
the white noise of you. here's to hoping my mirror
corner neighbors do not take out the trash any day soon.

Clinton Avenue

I vow to soak in each day I own.
every moment living an inch off
my young tongue. I dance on
numerous time zones. perhaps
this death is impending, for every
season has a finish line – will ours?
then again, the seasons do come
crawling back. returning to us all
through the sun cycles with ardent
loyalty. they always appear slightly
different, yet drenched in the same
basket of possibilities.

New York, my muse

blink
red to green
the traffic light
changes her opinion
my New York and
your New York
are different
beasts
perhaps they are
lovers
but they are
certainly
not friends.

Cooper Park

I return back to Cooper Park
to remind myself what I am
made of. underneath autumn
air, my bones appear to be
crafted from different magic
than I once believed in.
retraced footsteps leave me in
awe. I am out of my body and
on top of my back. I am light,
held by how I appear as a
stranger here. I sit on a bench,
but not *the* bench. I summon up
the many cycles of me. I search
for breath. sometimes I come to
remind myself of progress, to
evoke the bravery that slips away
in the darkness. other times I come
to let go. today, I let the wind decide.

the center of the universe

it is fall; I walk you up all six flights of stairs to see the skyline of our city from my home. somehow the waves of the building tops are ever changing and also, candidly unwavering. look closely and we see the life living inside. blink fast and we are back behind our own reality. breath on my neck, you say *every window has a story.* you are behind me, your front presses softly against my back. we stare at the building bodies. *I love to watch you watch the city,* you profess. palpably one of the most significant string of words to ever land on my shoulders. I hear my lungs confess into the night air how I cannot imagine a cause to ever leave. my mind has yet to envision it. I list off the endless ways I would not be swayed. I am fierce in my reasoning, squared away in my trajectory. now it is wintertime. suddenly, you are also home. the geography of safety lies on a body, not only on the ground. and just like that, it is springtime. I observe myself realize I would go anywhere with you. a belief brand new. covered with childlike innocence and possibility. a fantasy never before scripted in my brain. there has never been anyone or anything to unstick me from the avenues. to tear me from the pews of this religion. now my bones declare loudly, I would go to the woods with you. the mountains. the sea. the Shore. abandon the commotion and the rooftops for a rocking chair. a fireplace. a stack of books and hot tea. to fill the quiet with the sound of our songs. to paint a skyline with a stock of candle wax. the story in our slit of a window transcending the coordinates I once feared abandoning. today, it is summertime. I return back to my dear friend, the blissfully unchanged skyline I once gazed at with your body behind me. your body is surely not behind me. breathing in the heavy heat, I dig my heels deeper into the dirt than ever. I will wait for peace. for sweetness inside each hour. where I am held and all is right. I was once told New Yorkers live a hundred lives in a single day. I do not disagree. perhaps in the next one, a quiet porch will call my name and wish to rock with me, always.

I woke up to words today

I woke up to words today. on mornings
when my cup runs empty, at least I know
I will still come alive. every day inside this
city is a rebirth. it is a gift to hold such a
reliable notion in my chest. a stranger once
told me not to crack my knuckles. I confessed
to her I like the sound. I make myself known.

Klimt on 54th Street

rooted four feet from Gustav Klimt's *Hope II,* I weep.
I stand here for an unannounced measure of time. I
will never know how long I remain fixated. the docent
steps back, as one does. my heart is in pieces, but my
soul is whole. my mind is safe. my body is a pyramid,
far from fragile. tears crash to the ground. today I am
grown. my feet grip the marble floors as the voyages
that brought me here protect me. my past selves hold
me up - I can feel their palms wrapped beneath me. I
am made of all I have survived. energy soars out of the
soles of my feet, rippling down five floors into the city.
North and South of 54th Street, West and East of 5th
Avenue. the streets gather my lessons, nodding to the
life they have witnessed me build. the city corners call
out to each other, assuring one another that I can stand
without tipping. the streets blush, knowing the part
they played. today, I am one with Klimt's glimmering
pregnant woman. she bows her head, enveloped in a
multi-textured cloak. looking down on three faces far
beneath her, she appears content. safe. motherly. it is
said that the heads are either praying or mourning.
today I do not mourn. today, I lift my head. I sink into
my past selves that propel me and hope they live on to
multiply.

acknowledgments

I have never known a home like New York City, and perhaps I never will. However, it is not only the streets who have held me. I would not be who I am today and where I am today without the human guiding lights of my life. I am immensely grateful for my deep and true companions both inside of the city and outside of the city. Thank you to those who helped me craft my first home here, when I was just barely 22. Thank you to those who have since swept me off my feet and helped me to feel like I belonged, with no questions asked. Thank you to each and every one of you who has made various city corners such special coordinates, you know who you are. Thank you to the magical humans I have been lucky enough to meet inside the city walls, who are now my chosen family for life. And thank you to my real family, for letting me leave your arms and for loving me fiercely from afar – always. Thank you to Atmosphere Press for believing in my work, again. Thank you to Wingless Dreamer for publishing *a hotel room on Ludlow,* where it first appeared in an earlier form. And lastly, thank you to Metropolitan Avenue, 11th Street, and Second Avenue. If walls could talk, I hope you would be proud of how far I have come.

about atmosphere press

Atmosphere Press is an independent, full-service publisher for excellent books in all genres and for all audiences. Learn more about what we do at atmospherepress.com.

We encourage you to check out some of Atmosphere's latest releases, which are available at Amazon.com and via order from your local bookstore:

Poems for the Bee Charmer (And Other Familiar Ghosts), poetry by Jordan Lentz

Flowers That Die, poetry by Gideon Halpin

Through The Soul Into Life, poetry by Shoushan B

Embrace The Passion In A Lover's Dream, poetry by Paul Turay

Reflections in the Time of Trumpius Maximus, poetry by Mark Fishbein

Drifters, poetry by Stuart Silverman

As a Patient Thinks about the Desert, poetry by Rick Anthony Furtak

Winter Solstice, poetry by Diana Howard

Blindfolds, Bruises, and Break-Ups, poetry by Jen Schneider

INHABITANT, poetry by Charles Crittenden

Godless Grace, poetry by Michael Terence O'Brien

March of the Mindless, poetry by Thomas Walrod

In the Village That Is Not Burning Down, poetry by Travis Nathan Brown

Mud Ajar, by Hiram Larew

To Let Myself Go, poetry by Kimberly Olivera Lainez

about the author

Daniella Deutsch is a 27-year-old originally from Los Angeles, California. She migrated to New York as soon as she could, attending Skidmore College and is currently at NYU for her master's in Clinical Social Work. Daniella has had pieces published by online literary journals such as *Ink and Voices, Little Death Lit,* and *5x5 Literary Magazine.* Her print publications include, *In Parentheses, Gargoyle Magazine,* and *Wingless Dreamer Literary Magazine.* Daniella's debut book of poetry was published in late 2020, titled *all the things my mother never told me.* Daniella is a fierce lover of city rooftops, fresh pasta, packed concert venues, and the feeling of buying far too many new books on a whim.